ᛘ Contents ᛘ

♈ The Jewish ♈ Festival of Lights

HANUKKAH TAKES PLACE IN WINTER WHEN THE DAYS ARE SHORT. It lasts for eight days and every day candles are lit. It is a festival of lights.

LONG, LONG AGO

At Hanukkah Jewish people look back to a special time in their history. It is a time when they celebrate the triumphs of good over evil, weakness over strength and light over darkness. The festival dates back more than 2000 years. It reminds Jews of the time when they were living in Israel and the country was occupied by Syrians. God helped to free the Jews from the Syrians. This story is told in some Bibles in the books of Maccabees (see page 12), in the part called the Apocrypha.

A young girl lighting the Hanukkah candles on the last night of the festival

Candle decorations above a shopping precinct in Israel at Hanukkah

A WORLD OF FESTIVALS

HANUKKAH

HAPPY HANUKKAH

חג חנוכה שמח

HANUKKAH

Anne Clark
David Rose
Gill Rose

Evans

Evans Brothers Limited

Published by Evans Brothers Limited
2A Portman Mansions
Chiltern Street
London W1M 1LE

British Library Cataloguing in Publication data.

Rose, David W.
    Hanukkah. – (A world of festivals)
    1. Hanukkah – Juvenile literature
    I. Title II. Rose, Gill III. Clark, Anne
    394.2 67

ISBN 0 237 51802 3

First published 1998

Printed in Spain by G.Z. Printek

ACKNOWLEDGEMENTS

Editor: Su Swallow
Design: Raynor Design
Production: Jenny Mulvanny

The authors would like to thank Clive Lawton for his helpful
comments on the manuscript.

The authors would also like to thank the following institutions
and people featured in this book: Reform Synagogues of Great
Britain; Kingston, Surbiton & District Synagogue;
Wimbledon & District Synagogue; Wimbledon High School;
Alan Etherton; the family of Rabbi Hugo Gryn; the Clark
family; the Bower & Ish-Horowicz families; the Kahn-
Zajtmann family.

The authors and publishers would like to thank the following
for permission to reproduce photographs:

Cover Y Braun/Camera Press **Title page** Gitta Bechshoft,
Palphot Ltd/David Rose
page 6 (top) Deborah Gilbert/Image Bank (bottom) Trip/S
Shapiro **page 7** (top) Trip/S Shapiro (bottom left) Trip/R
Seale (bottom right) David Rose **page 8** (top) David Rose
(bottom) John Fortunato/Getty Images **page 9** (top) Trip/S
Shapiro (bottom left and right) David Rose **page 10** (top)
Ancient Art and Architecture (bottom) Museo E Gallerie
Nazionali Di Capodimonte/Bridgeman Art Library **page 11**
British Library/Bridgeman Art Library **page 12** (top) Genut
A.V. Productions (middle) David Rose (bottom) Ancient Art
and Architecture **page 13** (top) Robert Harding Picture
Library (bottom) Ancient Art and Architecture **page 14**
(top) Israel Government Tourist Office, London (bottom)
Trip/A Tovy **page 15** (top) Christie's, London/Bridgeman
Art Library (bottom) Trip/H Rogers **page 16** (left) Ancient
Art and Architecture (bottom) Robert Harding Picture Library
page 17 (top left) Trip (top right) Sarah Stone/Getty Images
(bottom left and right) David Rose **page 18** (left) David
Hanson/Getty Images (right) Getty Images **page 19** Naomi
Gryn **page 20** (top) David Rose (bottom) the Clark Family
page 21 (top and bottom right) David Rose (bottom left) the
Ish-Horovicz family **page 22, 23, 24, 25** David Rose **page
26** All pictures Genut A.V. Productions (bottom left) with the
permission of Macabi Organization (bottom right) with the
permission of International Chabad **page 27** Genut A.V.
Productions **page 28 and 29** Anthony King: Medimage

Page 19 extract by Rabbi Hugo Gryn taken from *Forms of
Prayer for Jewish Worship Vol III, Prayers for the High Holydays*.
Published by the Reform Synagogue of Great Britain 1985.

FAMILY FUN

Jews usually share this festival with their family, and children especially have a lot of fun. It is a time for lighting candles, playing games, singing songs, eating special foods, giving and receiving presents. When Jewish people meet, they wish one another 'Happy Hanukkah', or in Hebrew, 'Hanukkah Same'akh'. Hebrew is the language learnt by Jewish children around the world so that they can read the Bible in the language in which it was written and join in community prayers.

Jerusalem is the centre of the Jewish world. It is the capital city of Israel. The story of Hanukkah took place in and near to Jerusalem, where the Jewish Temple stood. Today all that remains of the Temple is the Western Wall, where many Jews go to pray.

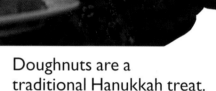

Doughnuts are a traditional Hanukkah treat.

Hanukkah decorations in a Jewish school. The Hebrew writing says 'Hanukkah Same'akh'.

Jews gather to pray at the Western Wall.

7

♈ Giving ♈ and receiving

DURING HANUKKAH CHILDREN receive small presents of money. They often get chocolate money, too! This gift is called *gelt*, the Yiddish word for money.

ALL KINDS OF GIVING

Nowadays all kinds of presents may be exchanged by the family. In some families children are given a small present each day of Hanukkah.

Another tradition at Hanukkah is that of helping people in need. This could be by giving of your own time and effort or it could be by giving money to charity. Helping others is called *tzedaka*. Throughout the year the Jewish religion provides opportunities for doing *tzedaka*.

▲ A Hanukkah present of chocolate money, which children use to play dreidel (see page 24).

◄ A Jewish family celebrating Hanukkah at home. Look for the *hanukiot* on the wrapping paper, and the lit candles on the table.

A Light in the Window

For each of the eight days of Hanukkah candles are lit in Jewish homes. The candle holder is called a *hanukiah* (plural: *hanukiot*). There are rules about how these are made, though they may come in various shapes and sizes and in different materials. Many families have a story to tell about their *hanukiot* (see pages 20 to 21). Some *hanukiot* are family heirlooms which are used each year and passed down through the family. Some *hanukiot* are home-made. In some families, each person will light their own *hanukiah* each evening of the festival. When the festival has begun, the *hanukiah* is lit by a window, so that it can be seen by everybody. *Hanukiot* are lit in the synagogue as well as at home.

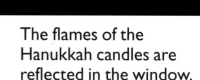

The flames of the Hanukkah candles are reflected in the window.

Some people send Hanukkah cards – children often like to make their own.

These young people are enjoying making and decorating their own *hanukiah*.

חנוכה שמח

HAPPY HANUKKAH

☥ A story of hope ☥

THE STORY OF HANUKKAH happened more than 2000 years ago in the second century BCE. For Jews around the world the story reminds them of a great triumph against all the odds.

ONE GOD

The Greek commander Alexander the Great had fought and won many battles in the Middle East. He brought with him Greek religion and culture. However, the Syrian rulers of Israel had allowed the Jews to follow their own religion. The Jews believed in one God, and built a magnificent Temple for God in Jerusalem, their most holy city. The Jews followed the teaching of the Torah, the Jewish holy book.

A mosaic of Alexander the Great in battle

Oriental Jews keep their Torah scrolls in beautiful cases.

MANY GODS

After the death of Alexander, King Antiochus came to power. He practised the Greek religion, which believed in many gods and worshipped images of these gods. He tried to make the Jews become like the Greeks. Some Jews did begin to follow Greek customs. Antiochus wanted to destroy the Jewish religion, so he forbade them to keep the laws of the Torah, such as observing the Sabbath. He put Greek idols in the Temple and put out the menorah, the special light which burned in the Temple and which symbolised the presence of God for the Jews. He commanded that pigs should be sacrificed as offerings to the Greek gods in the towns and in the Temple in Jerusalem.

To abandon belief in one God was against all the Jewish laws, but anyone who refused to obey was killed. Yet, many Jews began to rebel against the Syrians.

Find out how the Jews fought against the Syrians on the next page.

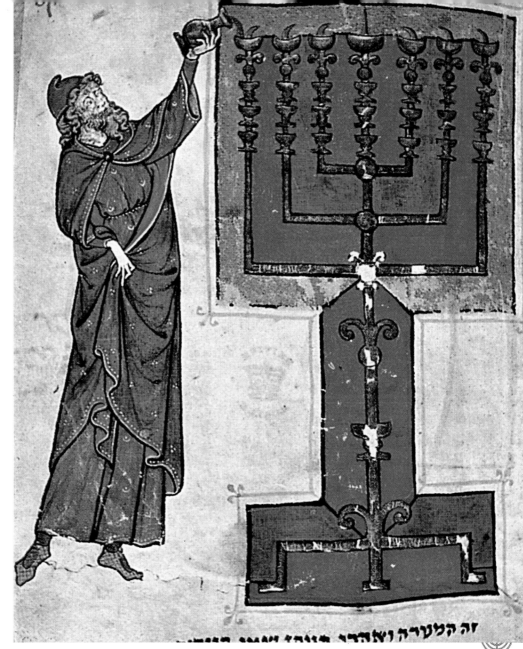

Aaron the priest, Moses' brother, pours olive oil into the menorah to keep it alight.

A battle and a miracle

THE JEWS HAD TO FIGHT A GREAT BATTLE against the Syrians, but they were few against many. How could they win?

ESCAPE TO THE HILLS

In Modi'in, a town near Jerusalem, a priest called Mattathias and his sons refused to sacrifice to the Greek gods and pulled down the altar to the god Zeus. They fled to the hills and were joined by other Jews who wished to remain loyal to their religion.

When Mattathias died, his son Judah the Maccabee took over. He led the Jews against the Syrians. King Antiochus was determined to destroy them. He gathered all of his soldiers together in a battle against the Jews. Though the Jews were greatly outnumbered, they won the battle. Judah led them into Jerusalem, where they began cleansing the Temple. They removed the images of the Greek gods and put an end to pig sacrifices, to make the Temple holy once more.

The countryside around Modi'in, the home of Mattathias and his family

A bronze head of the Greek god Zeus

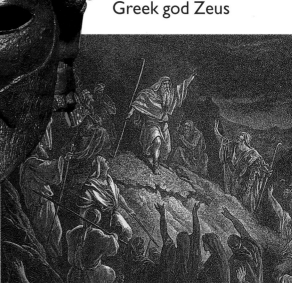

Mattathias encouraging the Jews to join in the struggle against the Syrians

This is a model of the Old City of Jerusalem, showing part of the Temple.

LIGHTING THE LAMP

When this was done the Jews wanted to re-dedicate the Temple to God and celebrate their victory. The menorah was lit once again. The Jews had found enough oil for the lamp to burn for one day. They knew it would take eight days to get new oil but they lit the lamp anyway. Then *a great miracle happened there* (see page 24) – the oil burnt for eight days!

From that time, each year Jews celebrate the festival of Hanukkah. The festival starts on the 25th day of the month of Kislev (in November or December). The story of Hanukkah is the first written record of people fighting for religious freedom.

Oil for the menorah in the Temple was made from olives.

♅ Hannah and ♅ Judith

H ANUKKAH IS A TIME WHEN the special contributions of women are remembered. The Talmud, a collection of Jewish teachings, says that 'women are obliged to light the Hanukkah menorah for they took part in the miracle.' Here are the stories of two special women.

A beautiful *hanukiah* in a museum in Israel

A WIDOW'S COURAGE

Hannah was a widow with seven sons. At the time when Antiochus was trying to stop Jews being loyal to God, Hannah encouraged her sons to defy Antiochus and remain true to God. One by one her sons were murdered until only the youngest son remained.

Antiochus tried to make the last son obey him but he refused. Realising how much it would mean to Hannah to lose her last son, Antiochus tried to persuade Hannah to make him change his mind. Instead Hannah told her son to remain true to his beliefs, and they both died.

Hannah's courage has been an inspiration to Jews at times of persecution.

Choosing a menorah as a souvenir of a visit to Jerusalem

SLAIN BY A WOMAN'S SWORD

A Jewish city was besieged by the Syrian army. A young widow named Judith left the city and entered their camp. When Holofernes, the Syrian general, saw her he was infatuated with her beauty and invited her to his tent. She prepared a meal for him, including cheeses to make him thirsty. He drank so much wine he fell asleep. As he slept, Judith drew out the sword she had hidden and cut off his head. She took the head back to her city.

Judith leaving Holofernes' tent, carrying his head by the hair

When the Jews saw this, they felt brave enough to attack the Syrians. Without their general to lead them the Syrians were easily defeated. To this day, foods made with cheese are often eaten during Hanukkah and this story remembered.

Greek cheese and spinach pie. Jews often eat foods made with cheese during Hanukkah.

♆ Light in the Temple ♆

HERE HAVE BEEN TWO JEWISH TEMPLES in Jerusalem over the past 3000 years. The first was destroyed by the Babylonians in the sixth century BCE. The second one was destroyed by the Romans in the first century CE. All that remains today is the Western Wall. But the light that burned in the Temple is still an important symbol for Jews.

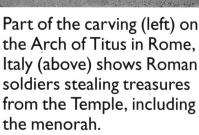

Part of the carving (left) on the Arch of Titus in Rome, Italy (above) shows Roman soldiers stealing treasures from the Temple, including the menorah.

A SYMBOL OF GOD

The story of Hanukkah is linked to the Second Temple. Inside the Temple was a huge seven-branched candle-

stick called the *menorah*. It was lit by oil and priests made sure it was always kept burning. The light was a symbol of the presence of God. This symbol is still used today. Every synagogue has a *ner tamid* (an ever-burning light) by the Ark where the Torah scrolls are kept. Nowadays these lights are likely to run on electricity instead of oil. The *ner tamid* reminds Jewish people of the original menorah in the Temple.

The menorah is the oldest Jewish symbol. Today it is the official emblem of the modern State of Israel.

A stamp showing the emblem of Israel – a menorah and two olive branches. The Hebrew writing says 'Israel'.

This giant menorah stands outside Israel's parliament building in Jerusalem. It was a gift to Israel from the British Government.

A stained glass window from a synagogue showing the destruction of the Second Temple

The *ner tamid* is always kept alight beside the Ark.

17

Hanukkah in the Holocaust

IN THE SECOND WORLD WAR Adolf Hitler and the Nazis tried to destroy the Jews living in Europe. Millions of Jews were imprisoned and killed, and others went into hiding to avoid capture. Throughout this period of the Holocaust Jews tried to keep their religious traditions alive, including the celebration of Hanukkah, which reminded them of earlier escapes from persecution.

A YOUNG GIRL REMEMBERS

In her diary Anne Frank, a young Jewish girl from Germany, describes how her family celebrated Hanukkah in the secret annexe, in a house in Amsterdam, in Holland. 'We didn't make much fuss about Hanukkah: we just gave each other a few little presents and then we had the candles. Because of the shortage of candles we only had them alight for ten minutes . . . Mr. Van Daan has made a wooden candlestick, so that too was all properly arranged.'
(The entry for Monday 7th December 1942)

The bookcase hides the entrance to the secret annexe where Anne Frank and her family lived.

Anne Frank, with an extract from her diary

Dit is een foto, zoals
ik me zou wensen,
altijd zo te zijn.
Dan had ik nog wel
een kans om naar
Holywood te komen.
Anne Frank.
10 Oct. 1942

(translation)
"This is a photo as I would wish myself to look all the time. Then I would maybe have a chance to

A Rabbi remembers

Rabbi Hugo Gryn, a leader of the Jewish community in Britain, wrote about his memories of the concentration camp during the war when he was a boy of 14 years old:

'It was the cold winter of 1944 and although we had nothing like calendars, my father, who was a fellow-prisoner there, took me and some of my friends to a corner of the barrack. He announced that it was the eve of Hanukkah, produced a curious-shaped bowl, and began to light a wick immersed in his precious, now melted, margarine ration. Before he could recite the blessing, I protested at the waste of food. He looked at me – then at the lamp – and finally said: "You and I have seen that it is possible to live up to three weeks without food. We once lived almost three days without water, but you cannot live properly for three minutes without hope."'

Hugo Gryn beside his mother, with his father and brother

Rabbi Hugo Gryn sitting in the garden where his mother buried family heirlooms, including their *hanukiah*, to keep them safe in the war.

⅄ Family stories ⅄

$\mathbf{M}$ANY JEWISH FAMILIES have stories to tell about their hanukiah, the candle holder that is lit at Hanukkah.

IN MEMORY OF A SOLDIER

This *hanukiah* belongs to Anne. It was given to her uncle, Kurt, for his Bar Mitzvah in Germany in 1932. Kurt managed to escape to England before the Second World War. He brought the *hanukiah* with him. Kurt volunteered to fight with the British army against the Nazis. He was very badly injured and never walked again.

Kurt spent a lot of time in hospital. He fell in love with the nurse who looked after him. Later on they were married. Kurt's wife is not Jewish. After Kurt's death, she gave the *hanukiah* to Anne so that it could be used on Hanukkah each year. This makes it very special for Anne and her family.

The *hanukiah* which Kurt's wife gave to Anne

Kurt in his army uniform (left), Anne with her husband David (below) and her twin sons Michael and Malcolm

A GIFT FROM AN UNCLE

This *hanukiah* belongs to Judith. It was made for her by her Uncle Meir who is very good at making things. Meir used to live in Poland. During the Second World War, Meir's new wife, his parents and other members of his family went into hiding. One day Meir heard that all his family had been betrayed and arrested. They were taken away and Meir never saw any of them again.

After the war, Meir went to Palestine, the country now known as Israel. He bought a machine which could make screw-threads and he worked for many years making brass fittings. When he retired, he sold the machine, but kept the old brass fittings and used them to make *hanukiot* for all his nieces and nephews. These are treasured and used every year.

The brass *hanukiah* which Meir made for Judith and her family

Judith and her husband Patrick and their four daughters

Meir with his great-niece

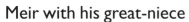

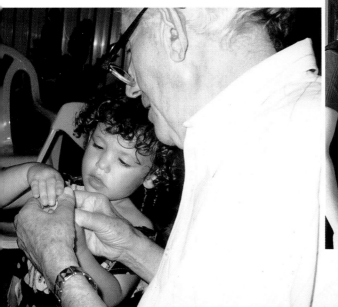

🕎 Food and light 🕎

URING HANUKKAH, WHILE THE
CANDLES OF the *hanukiah* are
burning, Jewish people enjoy themselves
and do not work.

An ornate oil-burning
hanukiah

POTATO PANCAKES

One way in which people enjoy themselves is to eat
special foods. Traditional foods eaten at Hanukkah
are doughnuts and special potato pancakes called
latkes. Latkes and doughnuts are eaten because oil is
used when making these foods and oil is a symbol of
the miracle of the first Hanukkah.

CANDLE CEREMONY

Hanukkah candles are lit at nightfall
on each of the eight nights of the
festival. The first candle is placed on
the right side of the *hanukiah* and,
each night after that, a candle is added
from the left. An extra candle, called a
shamash, or servant candle, is used to
light the other candles,
one on the first night,
two on the second night
and so on. Forty-four
candles are needed in all.

The candles are lit
from left to right, so that
the newest candle is lit
first. Then the servant
candle is put back in its
place in the *hanukiah*.

Sarah and her mother
making *latkes*

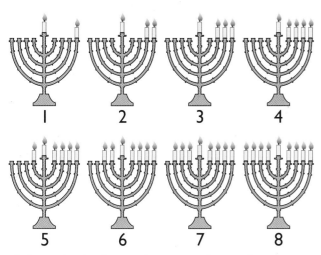

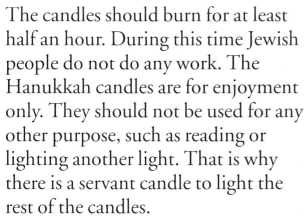

1 2 3 4

5 6 7 8

A *hanukiah* always has nine branches: eight for the eight days of the festival, plus one for the *shamash*. It holds candles or oil-burning wicks.

Sarah's brother Ben is lighting the *shamash*

The candles should burn for at least half an hour. During this time Jewish people do not do any work. The Hanukkah candles are for enjoyment only. They should not be used for any other purpose, such as reading or lighting another light. That is why there is a servant candle to light the rest of the candles.

This is the prayer that is said after lighting the candles:

'We light these lights on account of the miracles, the deliverances and the wonders which You performed for our ancestors by means of Your holy priests. During all the eight days of Hanukkah, these lights are holy, and we are not allowed to make any other use of them, except to look at them, in order to thank Your Name for Your miracles, Your deliverances and Your wonders.'

Sarah and Ben and their parents enjoy *latkes* and doughnuts.

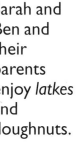

23

A festival game

ACCORDING TO LEGEND, THE GAME OF DREIDEL began when the Jews were ruled by the Syrians.

SILENT SECRETS

The Jews were not allowed to study the Torah nor observe Jewish holidays. They did so in secret. When they read the Torah or prayed they kept dreidels in their pockets. If the enemy came near they quickly hid their books and began to play dreidel. It then looked as if they were simply playing a game with a spinning top. This is how the Jews fooled their enemy.

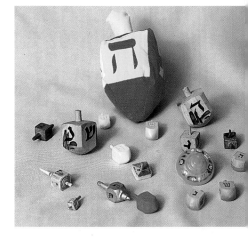

A collection of dreidels – there is even a soft one for babies!

PLAYING DREIDEL

The dreidel is a four-sided spinning top. Dreidel is a Yiddish word which means 'turn'. The Hebrew word for dreidel is *sevivon*.

There are four Hebrew letters on a dreidel:

Nun	Gimmel	Hey	Shin
(the sound 'n')	(the sound 'g')	(the sound 'h')	(the sound 'sh')

They stand for the words *Nes, Gadol, Hayah, Sham,* which means 'A great miracle happened there.' In Israel, the fourth Hebrew letter on a dreidel is *Poh,* so the dreidel says 'A great miracle happened *here,*' because the Hanukkah story took place in Israel.

The four sides of a dreidel from Israel

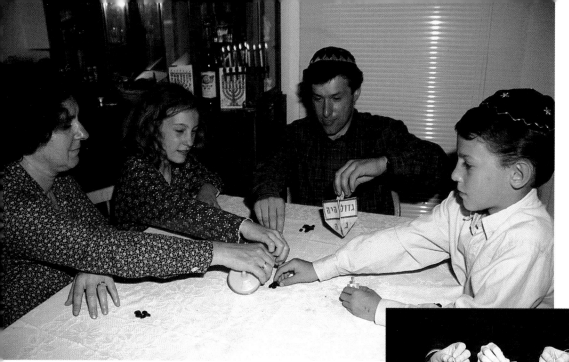

Sarah and Ben play dreidel with their parents.

Children at school show off the dreidels they have made.

THE RULES FOR PLAYING DREIDEL

All the players start with the same number of pennies, counters or raisins. They each put one in the middle. Jewish children often get a bag of chocolate money as one of their Hanukkah presents and use the coins to play the game.

◆ Everyone takes it in turn to spin the dreidel.

◆ If it lands on:

ג (Nun) you do **nothing**

ג (Gimmel) you '**grab**' everything in the middle

ה (Hey) you take **half**

ש (Shin) you '**sh**ove' one counter in

◆ It's the side of the dreidel facing upwards when it lands that counts.

◆ If the dreidel lands on Hey, and there is an odd number of counters in the middle, the player takes half of the total plus one.

◆ Before the next person spins, everyone puts in another piece.

◆ When someone has won everything the game is over. Alternatively, the winner can be the person with the most pennies, counters or raisins at the end of a set time.

25

♈ Bonfires and torches ♈

HANUKKAH HAS BEEN CELEBRATED in many different ways in different parts of the world.

In Modi'in, the home town of Mattathias and his sons in Israel (see page 12) a bonfire is lit at the tombs where the Maccabees are believed to be buried. A torch lit from that bonfire is carried by teams of relay runners all the way to Jerusalem. Flames from the Modi'in torch are used to light *hanukiot* at the Western Wall, the President's house and at other places in Jerusalem.

In Israel and elsewhere, giant *hanukiot* are placed and lit on buildings and in public places. This one is in front of the White House in Washington, USA.

A very modern *hanukiah* at the site of the Maccabean tombs

A runner carries the torch into a youth centre on his way to Jerusalem.

These Jews in Israel are celebrating Hanukkah with a picnic!

In Aden, Jewish children used to wear blue clothing on Hanukkah, because it reminded them of the colour of the heavens, and therefore of God who was responsible for the miracle of Hanukkah. In school, the children used to re-enact the Maccabean victory.

In Germany, on the last night of Hanukkah, people used to light all the left-over wicks and oil from their *hanukiot* in giant bonfires. They sang songs and danced around the fire, often until the early hours of the morning.

In Tunis, women would commemorate the seventh day of Hanukkah as the day on which the widow Judith killed the general Holofernes (see page 15). They would come to the synagogue and, for the only time in the year, they were allowed to file past the Torah, kissing it as they passed.

27

♈ Let's celebrate! ♈

J OIN IN THE FUN OF HANUKKAH! Make your own dreidel so that you can play the game shown on page 24 and make your own potato latkes for a feast at any time!

MAKING POTATO LATKES

This recipe will make about 10 latkes.

You will need:
1. 2 large potatoes
2. 2 tablespoons plain flour
3. 2 eggs
4. salt and pepper
5. oil for frying
6. a mixing bowl, whisk, frying pan and fish slice, potato peeler and grater

All you need to do is:
1. Peel and grate the potatoes.
2. Drain off any excess liquid.
3. Add well-beaten egg, seasoning and flour.
4. With the help of an adult, heat the oil in a frying pan.
5. Drop in spoonfuls of mixture, flattening it as you put it in.
6. When brown on one side, turn and brown the other.
7. Drain on paper kitchen towels.

MAKE YOUR OWN DREIDEL

You will need:
1. a copy of the dreidel pattern on thin white or pale-coloured cardboard (use the large template on page 31)
2. safe scissors
3. ruler
4. crayons or felt-tip pens
5. a glue stick (suitable for sticking paper and card)
6. a small pencil or thin stick about 13 cm long
7. a small blob of adhesive tack or Plasticine

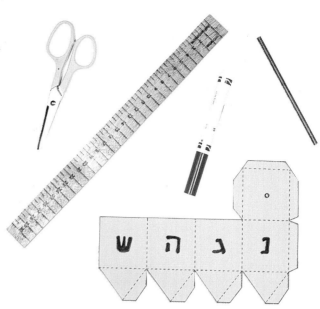

All you have to do is:
1. Carefully cut out the dreidel shape.
2. Make a small hole in the top where marked.
3. Colour the Hebrew letters. You can also decorate the outside of the dreidel with Hanukkah symbols, if you wish.
4. Score the dotted lines using scissors and a ruler. (You may need to ask a grown-up to help you with this).
5. Fold along all the dotted lines.
6. Stick flap at the side of the square.
7. Stick flaps at the base of the pyramid. Press the flaps into place from the top using the end of a pencil.
8. Poke the stick or pencil throught the hole at the top of the dreidel. Secure the bottom of the stick to the base of the dreidel using a blob of adhesive tack or plasticine.
9. Stick flaps at the top of the dreidel.

You can start playing with your dreidel as soon as the glue has dried.

Glossary

Apocrypha these books sometimes form part of an appendix to the Bible, they are not part of the Hebrew canon.

BCE Before the Common Era. The Jewish religion uses BCE and CE (in the Common Era) instead of BC and AD.

dreidel a four-sided spinning top used at Hanukkah.

Hanukkah an eight-day festival of lights celebrating the rededication of the Temple by the Jews.

hanukiah (plural: hanukiot) a nine-branched candlestick used during Hanukkah.

Hebrew the traditional language of Jewish scriptures and of many Jews.

latkes the name of potato pancakes usually eaten at Hanukkah.

Maccabee the family name of the leader of the protest against the Syrians. It means 'the hammerer'.

menorah the seven-branched candlestick lit daily in the ancient Jewish Temple in Jerusalem.

ner tamid means 'eternal light'. A light in the synagogue which is a reminder of the menorah.

shamash a 'lighter-candle' used to light the other lights on the hanukiah.

sevivon the Hebrew word for a dreidel.

Temple The focal point in ancient Jerusalem for Jewish worship. The house of God.

Talmud the oral traditions of the Jews were collected and written in the Talmud.

Torah means 'law' or 'teaching' and generally refers to the Five Books of Moses, the first five books of the Bible.

tzedaka helping others.

Western Wall all that remains today of the Temple in Jerusalem.

Yiddish a language spoken by some Jews. It is part German and part Hebrew, dating from the Middle Ages.

Index